How to Invest Your Money

Discover Everything You Always Wanted to Know About Stocks, Cryptocurrencies and Investment Platforms

Steven Moore

Table of Contents

Rolling Over Investments

It is said that you need money to make money. This belief stems from the idea that you invest a sum of money, and the proceeds then become a source of income. On the whole, this is a perfectly fine strategy. Of course, you need a sizable chunk of investment capital to make it work. This doesn't work well for those who don't have said investment capital.

Also, you need to ask yourself why you are investing in the first place. You see, most folks begin investing because they have a goal in mind. For instance, they are looking to save up for a down payment on a property, fund their retirement, or build the wealth they can pass on. All of these objectives, among others, are what motivate people to invest.

But one strategy that's commonly overlooked is known as "rolling over investments." This strategy is perfect for those who are starting small.

It should be noted that it's not the type of strategy that will build immediate wealth.

But it does is create a snowball effect that will eventually pay off in the long run. All you need is a little patience.

Rolling over investments consists of investing a certain amount and then reinvesting the entire amount repeatedly without withdrawing the original investment proceeds. In other words, you reinvest your principal plus interest. This is what creates the snowball effect.

The Snowball Effect in Action

Let's assume you start by opening a high-yield savings account and fund it with $100. Let's also assume that the bank pays you 1% monthly. This means that after the first month, you would have $101 (principal plus interest). Now, instead of withdrawing the $1 as income (on which you would have to pay taxes), you choose to roll it over for the next month. Now, the bank calculates your interest payout over $101 as opposed to $101. At the end of the following month, you have $102.01. The next month, you would rollover

$102.01 and make $103.03.

Do you see how the snowball effect takes place?

Sure, these numbers are underwhelming. However, they serve to illustrate how the snowball effect occurs when you choose to roll over your investments. This is a great strategy, particularly when you are not looking to make immediate use of the money.

How Much Should Be Invested

That depends on two factors.

First, it depends on how much money you can set aside. For most folks, money is tight. So, they may not be able to part with $1,000 to put away in a high-yield savings account, mutual fund, or ETF. Often, most folks start with less than $100. Ultimately, it doesn't matter how much money you start with. What matters is that you get started in the first place. Over time, you can add more funds to your investment and keep rolling it over. This makes the snowball effect grow even further.

Second, it depends on your aims. For most folks, investing is a means to an end. This means that they are not investing in the joy of investing.

Rather, they invest because they are looking to get something out of it. As such, they may not have an immediate need for this money. If that's the case, then rolling over your investments can be a great strategy for you.

Additionally, rolling over investment works well for those who are looking to build an additional fund.

This fund isn't destined to cover expenses or finance the acquisition of other goods. Rather, it serves as a savings fund, part of a retirement strategy, or simply as a means of protecting wealth. Thus, rolling over your investments makes perfect sense.

Investment Instruments to Consider

This boils down to your choice of an active or passive investment approach.

A very common approach is to set up a passive investment scheme in which you open up any type of investment accounts such as a certificate of deposit, high-yield investment account, mutual fund, ETF, index fund, or money market account.

Then, you put up your initial investment capital and simply let it roll over month after month. Depending on the type of account, you can add more funds to it whenever you can.

This last point is important as some accounts don't require much to open, sometimes as little as $25, but they ask for monthly deposits. This is important to note, as you may get penalized if you don't make the contributions.

If you choose this type of account, make sure that you can comfortably contribute the monthly contribution. Also, automate your contribution, so you don't even have to think about it.

Rolling Over Investments as a Tax Strategy

An overlooked aspect of investing is that you are on the hook for taxes on your profits. Any time you collect interest, you are liable for capital gains tax. Depending on the type of approach you are investing in, you may also be liable for income tax.

So, one of the best ways to bypass the entire tax song and dance is to roll over your investments. It's also worth looking into the specifics of the investment account you open. Some accounts require you to stay invested for at least three years. After the mandatory period, you can withdraw your money tax-free.

Depending on the nature of the account (and the balance), you can pull out sooner or must stay in longer.

In the case of 401(k)s or IRAs, you can't withdraw them until you are officially eligible to retire.

So, if you have one of these plans, particularly through your employer, then just let that money roll over and over. In the end, you'll stand to benefit a great deal once you are eligible to withdraw it tax-free.

It is certainly worth using rollovers as a means of minimizing your tax burden.

After all, you work hard for your money. So, you should be able to keep as much of it as you can.

Investing in Precious Metals

Every time there's talk of a recession or economic downturn, you hear about gold. This discussion centers on gold (along with other precious metals such as silver), being a hedge against downturns in stocks and other financial assets.

Indeed, gold is a hedge against downturns. This is mainly due to the inverse correlation between stocks and precious metals. The rationale is that when investors are uncertain about stocks, they pull their money from the stock market and sink into gold.

Aside from gold, silver, palladium, and platinum are all considered investment-grade precious metals.

These have a wide range in prices, making them somewhat unaffordable for investors that are just starting.

This is why many folks look to silver, as it is the cheapest of these metals. Additionally, silver tends to outperform gold. This means that when silver spikes, it short through the roof.

How to Make Money With Precious Metals

Firstly, you can buy physically and then sell for a profit. This is like buying and selling any other commodity. However, you need to be careful as buying and selling precious metals in pawnshops is not the best idea. So, this means dealing with a reputable precious metals dealer. These companies will happily buy-back your metals at a higher price. It all depends on the "spot" price, which is the metal's current market valuation.

However, you may find buyers that are desperate for physical metals. At this point, you can charge whatever you want for your position. This is why establishing a good relationship with a reputable dealer can turn into a profitable proposition when you are looking to sell your physical metal.

Secondly, ETFs provide you with exposure to the action, with much less risk and none of the stress. You make money if the price of gold goes up. You lose money if the price goes down. Depending on the nature of the fund, you'll get a check for your proceeds every quarter. Alternatively, you can ask your broker to rollover your proceeds. This makes your stake in the fund

Grow while avoiding any taxes on your earnings.

Making Money by Selling Your ETFs

In some instances, investors may be actively seeking to get into precious metals. However, sellers of physical metals may be in short order. So, investors would then flock to ETFs. This commonly occurs during economic downturns.

To make money in this situation, you can simply sell your stake in the ETF, not for the money you have invested but rather for the amount of money you stand to make.

Consider this situation:

You have invested $100 in a gold ETF. Investors are looking to buy into the fund you are invested in. So, you can sell your position for $200. The reason for this additional premium is that other investors are buying what your stake will be worth eventually, not what it is worth today. Investors are willing to pay this additional premium in desperate times when stocks are falling.

Please bear in mind that precious metals generally go in the opposite direction of stocks. So, when the stock market is tanking, your precious metals position should increase in value.

Physical or Paper?

There are two ways of owning precious metals.

The first is physical. This means that you purchase your metals and have them delivered to your home or office. This is called "allocated" ownership. The advantage is that you have complete ownership of your metals. Thus, you are the sole proprietor.

The downside is storing them in your home. This can get pricey. Besides, homeowner's insurance doesn't usually cover gold unless you add it to the policy.

The second is "paper." Paper gold means that you don't take physical ownership of the metal. All you are doing is gaining exposure to the market without ever getting ownership of the coins or bars. So, you pool your money, along with other investors, while a fund manager invests it in the metal. You then get a check every quarter for your earnings. This can be done

Through ETFs or gold investment accounts. The same can be done for the other precious metals. Alternatively, you can invest in a precious metals fund. This fund is diversified in all metals, thereby giving you access to all metals at once.

7691.08
7274.08
6857.08
14.37
13.12
11.47
16.02
17.27
6440.08
6023.08
5606.08
4772.08
4355.08

Beware of Premiums

When you buy physical metal, you must pay a premium. The premium is the amount of money paid on top of the spot price. This charge is issued to cover the dealer's expenses, overhead, and so on. Depending on current market conditions, premiums can range from a couple of dollars over the spot price to several hundred. It all depends on the price per ounce and the demand for it. Do your homework and shop around to get the best price.

It should be noted that when you buy into an ETF, there are no premiums to be paid as you are not purchasing the physical metal. Therefore, these premiums are not part of the contract. This makes your investment capital go further.

Precious Metals as Part of Wealth Preservation

There is a lot of discussions surrounding precious metals as a means of preserving wealth. If you are looking for a long-term investment, then this is the one for you. To preserve wealth, it makes sense to own physical bars and coins. The rationale behind this is that money loses purchasing power over time due to inflation. In the case of precious metals, their valuation keeps up with inflation as they are repriced over time. This means that the valuation of your metals goes up over time due to inflation. Thus, you get more money for the same amount of metals.

Precious metals can also be passed from generation to generation. It makes sense to keep them for a long time as coins and bars will not deteriorate with time. This is why they make great gifts. Plus, they are highly liquid. This means that they can be easily sold.

FOREX and Currency Markets

FOREX is one of the hottest markets at the moment; it is a dynamic, fast-paced environment. It is also the world's only 24-hour market. This means that you can trade on the FOREX market at any time you want. So, it's perfect for those individuals who are looking to make money in addition to their regular jobs. Moreover, those who make a living from trading FOREX have the opportunity to build a flexible schedule.

In essence, the FOREX market boils down to buying and selling currency. It's very similar to day trading, but instead of trading stocks, you're trading currency. Beyond that, the fundamentals are essentially the same. In general, the "buy low/sell high" logic applies here, as well. So, it's a question of playing the markets based on your expectations.

How Does FOREX Work?

Here is a sample FOREX deal you can make right away.

Let's take a look at a winning trade. In this trade, we're going to trade the currency pair USD/GBP. So, you are holding GBP and buy USD.

Here is the cross rate: USD stands at 0.84950 while GBP sits at 0.84960. Now, you decide to buy $10,000 as a part of the trade. Additionally, the USD/GBP pairing holds a margin rate of 3.34%. This is important as you are not required to come up with the $10,000 upfront. Rather, you only need 3.34%; in other words, you need to deposit $340 to finalize the deal.

Next, you need to sell your position before you get a margin call. This is why FOREX moves very fast. The longer you hold on to a trade, the greater your risk exposure. Thus, you need to be keen at which point you stand to make a profit. When you hit this point, you can sell for a profit.

In our example, the price shifts to 0.85540 for the GBP. So, when you sell, you stand to make about $15 on the trade. The result is profitable as you invested $340 and made $15 on the trade. This is a 4.4% return.

HFT in FOREX

Based on the previous example, you can make good money on FOREX by engaging in HFT. To make this work, you need to make multiple trades throughout a trading session. In short, the more profitable trades you make, the more money you earn.

Since FOREX is a 24-hour market, you don't need to trade at a specific time of day. You can trade at any time you free. There is no cap on the number of trades you can make in a session. So, if you make ten successful trades at $15 apiece, you can make $150 in a session. If you amplify that by 100 trades, you can make $1,500.

This is why HFT is the preferred approach to FOREX.

Moreover, the name of the game is automation. By automating your trades, you can make multiple trades in short order. The only time you need to invest in setting up your trades. Once you have them all in line, then you are ready to hit the ground running. As a result, FOREX is a great way to make profits with very little money upfront.

How to Get Started in FOREX

Like day trading, you need to find a brokerage institution to grant you access to their trading platform. Some institutions specialize exclusively in FOREX, while others may offer you access to FOREX through a regular day trading platform.

Ultimately, it's a good idea to find a day trading platform that allows you to trade FOREX. That way, you won't have to deal with multiple platforms.

You'll be able to trade in a single platform across various markets.

Additionally, this type of approach will allow you to learn about the system and perfect your strategy.

As for strategy, you can follow the top moneymakers in the FOREX world. These individuals post their picks on their sites. So, you can get free picks. Dailyfx.com is a great place to start. Their daily picks provide valuable insight. As a result, you don't need to put in hours and hours of research. You can follow their analysts' recommendations and place your trades accordingly.

Also, it pays to look into the amount of capital you need to fund your

Account. Most FOREX accounts can be opened with as little as $500. It's not a prohibitive amount though it may be a bit much for some at first. This is why tying your day trading account with a FOREX one can help you avoid this requirement. You might not be able to trade FOREX right away, but you are generally granted access to it after a trial period.

38.2%: 119.29
116.71
51.25%: 108.98
61.6 %: 99.19
104.19
86.72
72.48

FOREX ETFs

For those who favor a more passive approach, there are FOREX ETFs you can look into. They usually pay a higher yield as compared to other types of ETFs. However, these ETFs don't offer too many options. Therefore, you essentially invest your money and go along for the ride. Depending on the nature of the fund, you may be asked to keep your money in for several months before even seeing your first check. Unfortunately, FOREX traders take a lot of risks. Thus, they don't generally commit to making periodic payments or assign a fixed rate of return.

Nevertheless, FOREX ETFs can make sense for you if you are looking for a way to diversify your investment portfolio while trying to get away from stocks, bonds, or even precious metals.

The great thing about FOREX ETFs is that they don't require a lot of money upfront and allow you to contribute to the fund in a pay-as-go scheme.

In the end, you get a great deal of flexibility.

Overall, FOREX offers investors a great opportunity to make money in a very short time frame. So, if you are looking to make immediate returns, check out FOREX. While it won't make you rich overnight, it will provide you with the income you may need to cover your expenses in the short term.

Cryptocurrency Trading

Cryptocurrencies (or cryptos) are the latest investment that you can take advantage of. On the surface, the concept of crypto is rather straightforward. You can make money from trading crypto just like you would FOREX.

It should be noted that Bitcoin is not the only game in town. So, if you are keen on getting in on the action, there are thousands of other coins to choose from. Some cost pennies on the dollar. Hence, you can find some good value options.

So, let's take a look at how you can make money through investing in crypto with little upfront money.

Buy and Hold

The "buy and hold" strategy is one of the most common ways to invest your dollars. This strategy consists of buying up crypto and holding on to it for an extended time frame. It should be pointed out that the crypto is not nearly as dynamic as the FOREX one.

So, this means that you can't expect to day trade crypto and have the same results. Often, investors in crypto find themselves holding their positions open for several days, if not weeks, before seeing movements in price action. When this occurs, they can sell.

So, the buy and hold strategy makes sense, especially if you are looking to park some money that you don't need right away. However, there is one thing to look out for: the crypto market is highly volatile. This means that price changes can happen very rapidly. As a result, you could find your holding shoot up in value at a moment's notice. This is true of cryptos like Litecoin and Ethereum.

It is not recommended that trade in Bitcoin as its valuation is prohibitive for most investors.

Investing in Crypto ETFs

Crypto ETFs are a great way to get in on the action, especially when you don't have much money to start with. For some investors, purchasing a single

Bitcoin can be prohibitive. Considering that Bitcoin's price ranges from

$10,000 to $12,000 per coin, purchasing individual coins can cost a pretty penny. So, crypto ETFs provide investors with exposure to Bitcoin without shelling out the big bucks.

Making money with ETFs is pretty straightforward. You buy into the fund and see returns based on the amount you invest. The great way about making from crypto ETFs is that price can shoot through the roof at a moment's notice. As such, you can reap the rewards.

While ETFs are a passive approach, you can certainly make money over time by rolling over your earnings. Please make sure you are aware of the fund's rules as you may not be able to withdraw your money for some time. So do keep this in mind.

Trading Cryptos for Profit

This is the most straightforward way that you can make money with cryptos. In this strategy, you buy low and sell high. That's pretty much all there is to it. This is a more active approach and certainly favored by investors looking to maximize their earnings.

To make money from this strategy, you can start with cheaper coins. For instance, Litecoin trades about $50 to $60 a coin. This might seem appealing to you if you have about $1,000 that you can invest in. In that case, even a $1 increase in price would easily land you $100 profit straight up.

However, for some investors, $1,000 isn't realistic. So, there are even cheaper coins, like Tether. This coin trades at about $1 apiece. It's a great coin to get started. If you are looking for something even more affordable, XRP trades at about 30 cents per coin. With $100, you can buy a good chunk of this coin.

Realistically, you can make small profits in the early going. As the price increases, you can then turn around and make a decent profit. With a coin such as XRP, a gain of about 10 cents would make you a healthy return. Consider this situation:

You have $100 to spend on cryptos. So, you buy roughly 330 XRP coins at

30 cents apiece. Now, let's assume the price goes up to 35 cents per coin. When you sell your entire lot, you receive $116. That's a $16 profit on a single trade. Percentage-wise, that's a 16% return.

That's not a bad place to start.

High-Frequency Trading

From the previous example, you can engage in high-frequency trading. To make money in high-frequency trading, you essentially make smaller trades many times over. So, if you make $16 in a single trade and multiply that by 5, you could easily make $80 in a single trading session. Of course, this is assuming that you can pull this off five times a day.

In this example, we mention five times a day though it could be more. The great thing about cryptos is that there is a vast number of cryptos out there. So, you wouldn't necessarily make money from the same crypto over and over. Rather, you could make five separate trades in different coins. This would allow you to cash in several times a day.

Over time, you will learn the market so well that you'll know which coins to trade and when to trade them. In the end, you'll be able to build a steady stream of income.

Rolling Over Your Earnings

Just like with other types of investments, you can simply roll over your earnings. This will allow you to build up a greater amount of investment capital. As such, you'll be able to place bigger and bigger trades.

This, in turn, would help you generate greater profits in every trade. Ultimately, you will have the chance to generate enough income on a daily, weekly, or monthly basis to where you can rely on it. This stream of income is potentially unlimited.

So, you can't put a cap on how much you can earn.

Please bear in mind that many crypto investors like to combine high-frequency trading with the buy and hold strategy.

In doing so, you'll be maximizing your earning potential.

Shorting Stocks

Investors say a lot about shorting stocks. Many investors claim that it's too hard or too dangerous to pull off a successful short. This is true if you don't know what you are doing. However, if you have done your homework, you can make it work.

So, let's take a look at how you can pull off a successful short sale.

The Setup

Trade setup for a successful short depends on the direction a stock is trending. So, it's a matter of timing rise and the fall in price. It's not quite as hard as it sounds. But it does require you to be familiar with the stock's overall behavior.

To line up a good setup, you need to observe the stock's price action in question. Ideally, it should be trading in a range. That way, you have a predictable range on which you can base your setup. Since shorting a stock consists of selling it before you own it, you need to be sure that the price will rise to a certain point and fall back down.

When you are certain of these points, you can then move on to making the trade happen. The easiest way to determine if a stock is trading in a range is to observe its trendline. If you see the trendline moving sideways, then you know it's trading in a range. As such, all you need to figure out is where the resistance and support levels lie.

Making the Sale

Once you have identified the stock's range, the next step is to set up the sale. To make the short happen, you need to set up the sale first. This can happen by either buying an option or responding to another trader's request to purchase that particular stock.

Next, you execute the trade under the conditions of the buyer. It should be noted that you will have a specific timeframe to deliver ownership of the stock. During this window, you need to purchase the stock.

That way, you will own the number of shares needed to fulfill your end of the deal.

At this point, the trade hinges success on the price falling within the time window you have to deliver the stock. If this happens, you'll be able to buy at a lower price, thereby generating a profit. Should the price not fall, then you will still be on the hook for the stock. However, you'll have to buy it at whatever price it's available. You stand to lose money.

Making the Purchase

To make your purchase, you can set up an option based on the price you expect the stock to fall. If, and when, the stock falls to the level you expect, you'll be able to purchase it at a lower price than the agreed price. At this point, you can confidently buy the stock, deliver it to your buyer, and keep the difference.

If the price should not fall to a point where you can generate a profit, you can either cancel the sale (you can cancel the option) or go through with the trade and absorb the loss. Depending on the nature of the option, you may not be able to back out. So, you'll have no choice but to go through with the trade at a loss.

It's also important to note that if you fail to deliver, you could have your account suspended for a given amount of time, or you might be kicked off the exchange altogether. So, it's best to play by the rules in this type of trade.

Making a Profit

As you can see, making a profit is all about selling when the stock's price is at its highest point and then purchasing the actual shares when the price falls back down. The difference between the purchase and the selling price is your profit.

It should be noted that you don't need to have any money when shorting stocks. This is why it's quite risky to engage in this strategy.

If the price did not fall to where you expect it to, it would mean that you need to cover the difference from your funds. If you don't have enough funds, your account will be suspended.

If all goes well, you'll receive the proceed from the sale of the stock. Then, you can take these proceeds and purchase the stock at a lower price. Thus, you have enough funds to cover the spread. Many professional stock traders

Short stocks allow them to maximize the number of trades they make in a given period. Since they don't necessarily need to have the money to make trades happen, they can make multiple trades at once.

Sample Trade

Let's consider an example.

You are looking to short STX. This stock has been trading in a range between

$10 and $15 a share. You find an investor has taken out an option to purchase 100 shares. So, you make a deal with the investor to deliver 100 shares. At the time of the trade, you agree to deliver the shares at $15 each. That's

$1,500 that you receive from the sale.

The next step is to locate 100 shares of STX. So, you take out an option to purchase the 100 shares at $11 each. Another trader shows up and offers you the 100 shares at the price you requested. Thus, you make the deal, purchase the 100 shares for $1,100. Lastly, you deliver the shares to the first investor with whom you made the deal. You close the deal and keep $400 in profits.

In this example, it's evident that these types of deals can be made with no money. However, it's highly recommended that you do not short stocks you are not familiar with. Only short stocks you are very familiar with as you can ascertain where their price movements will go. This will save you a lot of headaches down the road.

Using a Robo-Advisor

In the age of automation, leveraging technology to your benefit is a must. Most of the trading in the stock market is done through computer algorithms and artificial intelligence. As such, that technology has made its way into the mainstream. So, it's no longer available to just big-time traders. Now, regular investors can take advantage of these incredible tools.

In this chapter, we're going to be looking at Robo-advisors and how these can help you maximize your profits.

The Science of Robo-Advisors

In essence, a Robo-advisor is a piece of fancy computer code that makes trades for you. Since there is no human interaction involved, the Robo- advisor can work for you as much as you want it to. You don't have to worry about it burning out or coming down with stress. It'll get the job done whenever you need it to.

Robo-advisors biggest advantage is that it requires very little maintenance once it's up and running. So, it doesn't cost much to make use of it; also, Robo-advisors have the luxury of processing vast amounts of information in a short time. Therefore, you can trust that it will make a smart decision based on available data. Of course, they're not perfect, but Robo- advisors, do have a much better track record than human traders.

Also, Robo-advisors can help you hit the ground running. This means that you can set up your account and start trading in a matter of minutes. As a result, you'll start seeing profits immediately. This means that all you need is to have your investment capital ready to go.

Cost of a Robo-Advisor

Naturally, a Robo-advisor is not free. In some cases, a Robo-advisor may cost around $25 a year. That's an incredibly low fee, especially when compared to the fees that stockbrokers charge. In some cases, your Robo-advisor may charge you a fee of 0.25% to 0.50% on the total balance of your account.

So, it pays to check out the terms of the account you are looking to open.

Additionally, trading with a Robo-advisor costs less than regular day trading. In day trading, you generally pay a fee per transaction. With Robo-advisors, brokerage institutions don't generally charge transaction fees. As a result, you make money on your deals without paying some of that back-in transaction fees. That's why you either pay an annual fee or a fee on your account balance.

Getting Started With a Robo-Advisor

Mainly, Robo-advisors deal with regular investment accounts such as the kind you open for day trading. Other types of Robo-advisors manage index funds or individual retirement accounts. They may even help you with your 401(k) portfolio. However, the bulk of Robo-advisors deal with individual trading accounts.

Some Robo-advisor accounts have a minimum requirement upwards of

$10,000. These types of accounts deal in specific markets and instruments. However, most Robo-advisors have very small account minimums. In some cases, you can open them for $500 or less. That's why it's important to check out various types of accounts.

Once you have selected your account provider, the Robo-advisor will assess your goals and risk tolerance. This is generally done by filling out a questionnaire. Depending on the nature of the Robo-advisor, it can be more or less thorough. Based on the information you provide, its trading algorithm will adjust its performance to suit your specifications.

Once the algorithm has been set up, the Robo-advisor will begin by selecting instruments, stocks, and other assets to fund your portfolio. Generally speaking, the Robo-advisor's algorithm will seek out the best choices among low-cost ETFs, index funds, or specific stocks such as those traded in the S&P 500. In other cases, it may copycat other algorithms.

This occurs when multiple algorithms are interacting with one another across various platforms.

What to Expect From a Robo-Advisor

If you already have a portfolio, you can enlist the services of a Robo-advisor to help you manage it. Often, balancing your portfolio is about managing risk or finding a balance among various asset allocations. Robo-advisors are good a diversifying your investments. As such, you can feel confident that your overall portfolio, regardless of your total amount invested, will respond to healthy parameters.

For instance, if your portfolio is invested fully in stocks, your Robo-advisor may whittle your stock allocation down to 25%. The remaining 75% may be spread across other types of assets such as ETFs, index funds, commodities, or FOREX. Ultimately, you determine the parameters the trading algorithm will follow based on your expectations.

Additionally, Robo-advisors are good at maximizing your tax-strategy. If you are looking for ways to help you manage your tax bill, Robo-advisors can provide you with a customized approach. Again, this depends on your specific parameters. Ultimately, you can get the right allocation based on your preferences.

A Hybrid Approach

A mix of a Robo and human advisor can provide you with a solid two-pronged attack in some cases. This strategy is useful, particularly when you are looking to be a passive investor. It should be noted that this approach is generally reserved for individuals with a larger portfolio.

A hybrid approach is generally reserved for investors who have at least $25,000 worth of investable assets. Companies like Charles Schwab, Vanguard, and Facet Wealth all offer these services. Nevertheless, you can check out the strictly Robo-advisor services. They start with as little as $500 in investment capital. If you choose to roll over your earnings, you can build up your investment capital quickly.

This is important to note as Robo- advisors tend to outperform the market. So, it's worth considering.

Lastly, using a Robo-advisor is a good strategy for combining it with other investment approaches. For instance, you can combine your Robo-advisor along with day trading.

Please bear in mind that the more income streams you can generate, your overall portfolio will be better. So,

Robo-advisors are a low-risk, high-reward proposition you should look into.

Trading With Acorns

Acorns is an automated investment fund. This fund was developed by a group of investors, Ph.D. economists, and software engineers to provide investors with an easy way of saving money for retirement. Since its inception, Acorns has grown to a one-billion-dollar fund. It has been quite successful.

Getting Started With Acorns

Acorns used the concept of "micro-investing." This means that you do not need a large amount of investment capital to get started. You can get started investing with Acorns with as little as a dollar. You can then add money to your account as you go. There are no account minimums and no fees. This is why Acorns is such a great alternative for those investors that don't have much money to invest.

Since Acorns is a fully automated system, all you need to do is set up your account. It takes about 5 minutes, and you're all set to go.

The system takes care of the rest. Acorns invest its funds in a myriad of diversified assets. So, it's about as safe as stock investing can get.

Your Acorns Portfolio

Your Acorns portfolio is one large, collective portfolio shared among all other investors who are part of the fund. As such, both the risk and wealth are spread out among all of the fund investors. When you set up your account, you'll be asked to fill out a questionnaire much the same way a Robo-advisor does. This helps the trading algorithm determine the best options to build your strategy. Therefore, your returns are based on the amount of money you have invested. So, if you invest a dollar, your returns will be calculated on that dollar. Additionally, your rate of return will be based on your expectations.

This makes Acorns a practical way of making money generate more money.

Acorns is a great way for you to get started with saving and investing with practically no money.

You can get started with a dollar. However, it would be best to set aside a larger amount, say, $20 or even $50.

In the passive form of investing, all you need to do is set up your account and watch your share of the portfolio grow.

That's all there is to it!

Building on Your Initial Investment

Once you have made your initial investment, even if it's just a dollar, you can then add to your account as you go. Since there are no account minimums, you can add as much money as possible to your account. Acorns are about investing your spare change.

This means that you can put as much money as you can into the fund. Additionally, there are no penalties if you don't add any more funds.

Consider adding a fixed amount every week, or month, to your account to make your investment grow. This will help your investment gain momentum. Since you can add as much, or as little, as you wish, Acorns gives you the flexibility of converting it into your digital piggy bank.

Rolling Over Your Earnings

The next step is to take your earnings and roll them over. Since micro- investing starts quite small, it's best to roll over your earnings on top of what you add to your account. This enables you to create a snowball effect. As the snowball grows, you'll be able to watch your funds generate more and more returns. As a result, you'll soon see your money growing like magic.

Please beware of a common mistake most novice investors make by pulling out their investment too soon. Often, investors get anxious and pull their money way too soon.

In this case, their investment doesn't have the chance to snowball into a significant sum. As a result, they feel the investment wasn't worth it.

So, investing with Acorns is about putting spare change into the digital piggybank and then forgetting it. Furthermore, you can automate deductions from your bank account. Given that there are no limits, you can automate as much as you want. This makes investing in Acorns even easier.

The Purpose of Investing in Acorns

Investing in Acorns is a great way of building an emergency or rainy-day fund. Lots of folks find themselves without a fund they can draw on in case of emergency. Since saving money in a regular piggybank doesn't generate any returns, it's can be tough to build a fund the old-fashioned way.

With Acorns, you can build your emergency fund very quickly, easily, and without any of the hassle. Before long, you'll have enough money set aside should you ever need it.

Consider this example:

If you invest a dollar at a 5% monthly return, you'll ear a nickel on that dollar every month. That's a nickel you have earned by simply opening an account and depositing that dollar. The next month, you'll earn 5.25 cents just by rolling that one dollar over.

If we expand this example to $100, you'd be making $5 a month. By rolling over your investment, you stand to make $5.25 the next month, and so on.

This is why it's best to leave your money in the account so you can allow it to gain momentum. As such, investing in this type of account is about starting small and letting your seed grow consistently. Eventually, you'll hit your target.

Over time, an investment account in Acorns can provide you with a significant source of income. Ultimately, this depends on your lifestyle. If you live a relatively modest lifestyle, it shouldn't be too tough to build a solid income stream. While it may not pay for everything, it will certainly help you to supplement your overall income. It can provide you with the opportunity to generate passive income.

So, it is certainly worth taking a chance on Acorns. You'll be glad you got started in micro-investing.

Investing in Index Funds

Index funds are another great passive investment. They provide investors with the opportunity to gain exposure to the stock market without trading in individual stocks. This is an important feature as it helps diversify risk. On the whole, index funds give investors exposure to an entire stock index, that is, a whole array of stocks. As a result, this diversification mitigates risk. This is the ultimate way of putting your eggs in various baskets.

Getting Started With Index Funds

The first step is to select the right fund for you. There are several funds. So, it's important to review them all before setting your sights on one.

Here is a list of the major ones:

The Wilshire 5000

The Russell 2000

The NASDAQ Composite

MSCI EAFE (mostly European and Asian stocks) The Dow Jones

There are also other smaller stock indices. The smaller ones tend to be custom-made products set up by financial corporations or hedge funds. They are pitched to individual investors or may represent a specific niche. You can look into these if you are keen on investing in a smaller fund. However, these funds may require higher investment capital. So, it's important to keep that in mind.

Index funds are pegged to a specific stock index. For instance, Dow Jones groups the 30 largest companies in the United States. In comparison, the Wilshire 5000 is based on the 5000 largest corporations. This implies that there is a much broader selection of companies.

+12.32%
+41.87%
+63.45%
+32.69%

Making Money With Index Funds

Buying into an index fund can be done in one of two ways. The first way is through an online platform, such as in the case of day trading. In this case, you select your fund and buy into it. Depending on the fund, the minimum

The amount of investment capital will vary. In some cases, you can buy into the fund with as little as $200 or $300. With these funds, you'll find that they offer moderate returns. Roughly speaking, index funds perform at the market average. On the whole, you can expect a run-of-the-mill fund to perform at around 6% a year.

That's much better than the returns you'd get on a regular high-yield investment account.

Thus, you make money as long as the market is up. If the market experiences a downturn, as you would expect to from time to time, then you may end up losing money. This is why index funds offer good value as they are invested across a wide range of companies and industries. Unlike industry-specific ETFs, index funds look to spread out your asset allocation as much as possible. This is how you can achieve these returns.

All About Fees

It should be noted that index funds come with fees attached. These fees are generally charged for account maintenance. This is true of funds that human money managers manage. Naturally, the institution issuing the fund needs to cover overhead. If you are keen on having a human money manager handle the fund, this would be the best option.

However, there are index funds that are managed by Robo-advisers or trading algorithms. As such, they don't require any human interaction.

These funds offer a great deal of value as they charge minimal maintenance fees. In some cases, they don't charge any fees at all. So, it's worth looking into an index fund managed by a Robo-advisor. Often, automated fund managers beat average market returns. So, this bodes well for you.

Setting Up Your Strategy

When you go about setting up your strategy, there are two possibilities.

The first is the "buy and hold" strategy. This is a long-term strategy that you can use if you aren't in a rush to make significant returns. This approach is highly passive and capitalizes on the snowball effect. In short, the longer you leave your investment intact, the more money you make. Also, you can simply roll over your investment every time the interest payout comes around. If your fund offers monthly payouts, then simply roll them over. If interest payments are quarterly, you might consider pulling a portion of it and rolling over the rest.

The great thing about the buy-and-hold strategy is that it doesn't take a lot to get started. You can begin with whatever the account minimum happens to be. Then, you can add more funds to the account as you can. Over time, you'll see your investment begin to take off.

The second approach is a much more aggressive one. In this approach, you open up your account with the minimum required. Then, you commit to putting as much as you can into the fund.

However, you are not looking to buy and hold for the long haul. When you choose to take a more aggressive approach, you need to be ready to pull your money when the market is heading toward a recession. As a yardstick, the stock market enters "correction" territory when it's down at least 20% from its previous high.

Taking 20% is not a good investment. Consequently, you need to be ready to pull your investment as soon as you see trouble ahead.

To facilitate your chances of pulling out ahead of time, you need to make sure that there are no time restrictions. Some funds may ask you to keep your money invested for a certain time frame.

If this is the case, you might be on the hook for a few months or even a few years. If the markets take a downturn during that time, you have no choice but to go along for the ride.

However, if you have the freedom to pull your money as soon as trouble looms, you can do so freely. Then, you can reinvest once the crisis is over.

As you can see, index funds are a great way to enter a passive investment without having to make a significant upfront investment.

Investing in Private Equity

When we refer to private equity, we're talking about taking an ownership stake in a private company. This means that you are not buying stock from a company that's traded on the stock market. Rather, you are investing in individual companies such as startups.

Investing in private equity generally involves funding a new company or providing startup capital. In most cases, this requires a significant investment, often thousands of dollars.

Now, it's important to note that private equity means that you receive shares, or a stake, in a company in exchange for your cash.

So, let's take a look at how you can make money by investing in private equity.

Taking Part in Crowdfunding

Entrepreneurs turn to crowdfund when they need capital. This capital can be used for any number of aspects related to the business. Since finding individual investors that can provide them with capital is hard, some entrepreneurs turn to crowdfund.

In these crowdfunding campaigns, entrepreneurs usually offer incentives to their investors. For instance, they'll offer limited-edition products. In other cases, entrepreneurs may choose to issue stock in exchange for funds. These are the types of opportunities you can take advantage of.

During some crowdfunding campaigns, entrepreneurs may put up a few thousand shares at a specific share price. Depending on the price, you can buy up a bunch of them. In other cases, shares may be so cheap that you can buy up a decent lot for a couple of hundred dollars.

Making money in this type of approach is rather straightforward. You can hold on to the stock until the company begins to expand and take off. At that point, you might get a buy-back offer from the founders of the company. At that point, you can sell for a profit. Otherwise, you can sell to other investors later on.

Taking Dividends

If you choose to hold on to the stock, you should be eligible to take dividends. Dividends are the portion of the profits that shareholders are entitled to. Since you were generous enough to invest your money in a given company, you should get a cut of the proceeds.

However, you need to be careful. Please ensure that the terms and conditions of the stock issue state that you are eligible for dividends. This is important to note, as the terms may state that you would be eligible for dividends after a specific time frame. Therefore, you need to be aware of this before pledging your money.

Still, taking dividends can be a great way of adding another revenue stream, especially if you aren't in a hurry to see a significant return on your investment.

Scoring on an IPO

Some startups take off to the point where they choose to go public. When a private company goes public, an event known as an Initial Public Offering (IPO) takes place. A fixed share price is set based on the number of outstanding shares and their valuation during an IPO. If you were fortunate enough to get into this company before it took off, chances have you scored shares at a very low price. By the time the company is ready to go public, shares would be worth a lot more.

The way you make money here is by selling your stake once the company has gone public. However, you need to do your homework. Investors who sell right at the opening of the IPO may end up missing out on massive profits.

Generally speaking, companies soar in the days following the IPO. In that event, you could make a killing.

However, not all companies soar following their IPO. Some pullback before taking off. So, the safe bet is to sell right at the start of the IPO. This is the most effective way of ensuring a good return. This is the ultimate buy-and-hold strategy for private equity.

Cashing in on a Takeover

There are cases in which larger firms take over private companies. When this occurs, shareholders are bought out entirely. In general, the founders retain some interest in the company (it's usually a token gesture), while the rest receive their fair share.

Much like an IPO, when a private firm is bought up, it is valued based on its financials and earning potential. This valuation is then divided by the number of outstanding shares. It's at this point where investors clean up. There are cases in which the larger corporation may be willing to pay a premium on top of the share price as a means of getting the deal done.

The Key Is to Get in Early

Most startups do several rounds of financing. In the early going, crowdfunding is one of the easiest ways in which entrepreneurs can raise capital. It can be very hard to attract venture capital firms in the early days. So, smaller investors may find a good opportunity to make a significant investment. Thus, the key to making money in private equity is to get in early.

The caveat here is to make sure you avoid sinking in too much money into a single company. This is important as most companies don't pan out over the long-term. In some cases, you'll get your investment back. In the worst of cases, you'll miss out.

Most of the time, you'll make a modest profit.

So, it's important to keep in mind that private equity is about holding your stake for an extended time frame. It might be a matter of years before you see a significant return. But if you happen to hit a home run, it will be worth the while.

There are three things to look at when you plan on investing in private equity:

1. The market for the products and services of the company
2. Sales projections for at least five years
3. The company's track record

If a company fails to produce any of these three items, pass on it. Any company you plan to invest in should at least produce some kind of track record that can back up their claims. Otherwise, investing in an untested company may be nothing more than wishful thinking.

indexes - day, 5
61.81%
indexes - day, 12
50.00%
38.19%
indexes - day, 144
23.88%

The Anatomy Of Dividend Investing

The holy grail of investing has been searching for and achieving a reasonable return rate on one's assets. This may be a struggle to neutralize risk at a reasonable yield despite relatively low-interest rates and a wide variety of investment options.

While not as trendy as a hedge fund or "exciting" as selling options, investing in companies paying rising dividends is a solid foundation for anchoring the investments. We assume that the cornerstone of the investments will be high-quality dividend stocks. Why? Why?

1) Research has shown that such payout securities are reliably cheaper in the long run than other securities. Approximately 30 percent of cumulative portfolio returns are made from dividend payers.

2) Throughout the years, they have a growing influx of revenue. Each year, that's a salary raise!

3) We also sell mere growth stocks in today's competitive markets to cover verse rates.

4) We put together four main points to help you grasp the highest performing businesses' structure for dividends. You will be able to find, pick, and extend your dividend portfolio by following these criteria.

The Root Of The Matter-Dividend Growth

The lifeblood of dividend income is dividend development. Inconsistency may be a symptom of a problem, much as in the heart rate. The same refers to transactions in payout securities. The cohesiveness of the dividend increase is the main factor. While the same figure will rise year after year, it is more critical to be raised by a constant number every year. Our rule of thumb is to search at businesses with an annual 5-7 year growth of 7-10 percent. Instead, after it, the organization offers you a pay boost per year. It was lucky that our employer lifted 2-3 percent-especially in this environment, to most of us.

The Muscles Vs. Fat The Payoff Ratio

It appears like Hanz and Franz, but note, weight is still significant. This can have its benefits (so that you can show off your "muscled" body, with facial expressions shouting "Pump [clap} you up").

Why? Why? When required, the body turns fats into sugars to provide strength. If you like, a contingency found.

The same refers to dividend distributions. Sure, just not at the cost of comprehensive employment. You want money. Put specifically, the distribution ratio is the number of dividend profits.

For example, a business receives $2 and gets a dividend of $1, and it has a 50 percent payout ratio.

By understanding the firm's dividend payment ratio, you can stop purchasing stocks whose profit is too small, and most specifically, unsustainable.

Which is to be avoided?

- 75% or higher tier
- 30% or a smaller amount
- Inconsistent compensation rates

Buying such securities typically contributes to a lower yield, accompanied by reduced product costs and, finally, a buyer's remorse.

We tend to identify businesses with a profit level between 40% and 60%-the perfect spot.

This offers the owners a good return while maintaining enough capital to fund expenses, grow the company, and increasing the dividend (pumping up the earnings).

A Strong Business

Well, it's about dividends development, as dumb as this can sound. Not a hot new inventory or drug. While you want to invest money, this approach is more about the return, year after year.

The third critical point, since contemplating an enterprise's dividend growth strategy and distribution ratio, is the company's coherence across the economic cycle.

This is where "fad" goods and services and businesses "dying" try to be stopped. Buggy whips, CB radios, and Pogo sticks were not checked despite being revolutionary and famous in their day. Boring is a positive thing here.

I like to see businesses that will market their goods ten years from now at better rates irrespective of the economic cycle.

Don't Sell The Stocks.

Even because stuff often doesn't fit in a personal partnership. And yes, it can be challenging to break up, but generally, it turns out to be the right thing. The same goes for owning a stock.

It's all right to "like" your inventory, but don't fall in love with it. Emotion and money do not destroy your spirit, but your pocket certainly does crack. Learn the signals that things are shifting. Earnings, for example, are that (one missing quarter is ok), but not an overall structural improvement.

Often the economy offers you the chance to earn faster than you expected.

Although we are not in favor of selling, it is prudent to remove some of the benefits off the table if the stock has significantly risen in a limited time (say 40 percent in six months).

The same is accurate at the edges.

When a stock declines 20%, and the basics are still fine, adding more to the fund is smart.

But, if things get wrong with the firm's sector, sell your place and search for other opportunities.

As our parents claimed, there's a lot of fish just in the water.

While not as comprehensive as Grey's Anatomy, our anatomical dividend investment framework would encourage you to diagnose your portfolio informally.

The aim is to draw on a plan, the methods, and the practice. This is the best thing about the business; it still offers chances for buying or selling.

Buybacks Or Dividends: Which Are Good For Shareholders?

Savings and equity buybacks are commonly used as a means for a company, as practical counterparts, to "return the money" to its shareholders. However, they are not at all equivalent.

Indeed, the only link between dividends and equity buys is that the corporation requires a part of its profits to pay for it. When you are a client, it is the capital that the company controls.

The Critical Stock Investor should not be oblivious to the mechanism by which it uses to return its shareholders' money. See what the gaps are and determine for the Rational Equity Investor what is better.

Dividends are straightforward: the corporation sends you the money.

Dividends are always declared quarterly, approved by the Board of Directors, and forwarded a few weeks later to the shareholders.

The Board claims that the payout is $1.00 per vote. They send you $100 if you have 100 shares. What would be more straightforward?

Share buybacks are often not complicated, nor more than dividends. In the case of stock repurchase programs, the Board permits the company's retained earnings to buy shares of the company on the open market.

The plan may be that, for example, the company would buy 1,000,000 shares in itself in the next six months and take them in and out of the market.

If the stock during the plan sells an average of $20 per share, the company pays

$20,000,000 to purchase its shares.

Why are these two very different actions, often referred to as similar ways of "giving money" to shareholders? In principle, the company uses part of its remaining profits to transfer the interest to its owners.

With dividends, capital itself is "something of value." The organization will give you a report.

The "something of value" comes with the buyback of the share in the form of an increase in each market share value. When the company buys X shares, the remaining (theoretically) shares are worth more to its holders. The corporate cake has been divided into smaller and, therefore, marginally larger pieces.

The cumulative number of outstanding shares reduces, meaning that each remaining stock is a higher percentage of the company, a slightly higher yield on its potential profits.

All right, say you're a business owner.

Will you be worried about the direction the organization uses to give you "any value?"

Here are the benefits and the reverses of the dividends:

- Pro: They are the right money in your wallet. It's all for the abstract.
- You can invest that money in the company again or do anything you want. You can use it as revenue.
- Pro: Most dividend programs are corporate policy equivalents. Companies never slash or delete dividends. While each dividend payout is a different case, the overall scheme is sacrosanct at most businesses paying dividends.
- Pro: Dividends help support a higher share price, provided a substantial dividend program worth on the market. Research demonstrates that the market puts interest on dividend schemes over long stretches.
- Dividends are closely monitored and reported, so it is easy to get information. Over time, companies establish pretty predictable dividend patterns. Critical trend shifts are recorded immediately.

- Con: You have to pay dividend taxes. However, the 15 percent federal income tax limit on distributions makes it one of the least taxable income sources available.

Below are the advantages and drawbacks of share purchases:o pro: Because you don't get money, you are not taxable.

- Pro/con: The repurchase of shares decreases the number of shares available and increases the remaining stock's worth. To understand this improved interest, however, the company needs to update the remaining shares.
-

You are abstract only if and when this occurs.

- Con: You're not sent any money. When you want the value of the capital, you have to sell any of your shares. The income you receive from the sale is then charged at the rate of capital gains, either on a long or short-term basis (as long as the transaction is more costly than the shares you initially paid).

The long-term government limit is 15%, the same as for distributions. The short-term limit is the most likely higher marginal tax rate.

- Con: Stock repurchase schemes of most companies are "one-offs" and not healthy. Scale or size are not reliable.
- Con: Stock buyback schemes are not closely supervised. Most of them are never done until their first release. Inconsistently, these errors are published in the financial press.
- Con: Most businesses buy back shares and repay their executives (and other staff) on equity incentive awards. The executives turn around and promptly refund the shares to the company as they are included in their pay plan. Therefore, the equity buybacks of the corporation are insurance expenses for the client. The managers, not the owners, get the money.

- Con: Stock repurchases are always made at the lowest share price. The initiative should be rolled out in reaction to a surge of income, which contributed to a higher share price in the market. That may also be that the corporation now wants the shares to pay for decisions that the corporation can not manage.

Unfortunately, management works in many companies that profit more than shareholders, although the shareholders are the company's owners. How is this happening? For a big, multinational corporation - whose fiduciary responsibility is to protect the owners' long-term interests - the Board of Directors is also hostage to management.

Management proposes, and the Board does not carry out its supervisory function effectively. It comes at the center of too many financial controversies over the past decade.

Compare that with a private corporation. Many of these corporations may be very broad, but their ownership is not so different from that of a publicly-owned corporation. In such a company, the company works for its founders- who often sit on the board. The Management Council is not in isolation, and management is a slave of the Council as it needs to be. For these businesses, you assume that significant dividend distributions are part of the package for the founders. Dividends remain well ahead of sales, as business earnings say. Whatever income is not required to finance ongoing activities or extension is directly passed to the sellers. When you are the sole owner of a business, wouldn't you?

Therefore, if one of the financial goals is current profits, dividends will now be more attractive than equity repurchases. They come regularly (and are often increased); they come in cash format, which is income at once; they are taxed at a low rate, and they do not require you to sell shares to realize what "valuations" are transferred to you. Moreover, the fact that management retains a robust payout policy shows that the business is run for its owners' well-being rather than by command.

The administration is expected to make wiser decisions on remaining earnings (after payment of dividends), which will favor you as a long-term investor.

Dividend Stocks Outlook Yield High

The Federal Reserve has stated that it plans to hold historically low-interest rates for a long time, and inflation looks to be under pressure. The results in the first quarter will turn up well in contrast to anemic estimates in the end. Retail revenues seem to be returning when we exit the slump. Unemployment has declined and may also marginally decrease. The aggregate economy has been recovering significantly since the lower months, and large sums of cash are also on the brink of coming back into the business.

On the other hand, our national debt has risen to an alarming pace with introducing the stimulus program at a terrifying rate. Middle Eastern geopolitical instability also remains crucial as we are now in two conflicts and have ongoing nuclear issues with Iran.

While Al-Qaeda is searching for new safe areas to meet in Syria, we see growing problems. Global warming problems remain unanswered.

The world's ambitions to come to some collective consensus, as demonstrated by the "non-results" of the Copenhagen meeting on dealing with it.

Our Government is also worried that too much debt would jeopardize our ability to continue paying loans by exporting treasury bills to India, Japan, and other foreign front countries.

Interestingly, we consider a second stimulus package to ensure that we do not slip into stagnation, given these fears. In general, the crystal ball our economists look into the future can be a bit more blurry than average because what is going to happen is tough to foresee.

And what does that mean for stocks with high yield dividends?

It's still lovely, as they say, to predict the best and plan the worst case.

If 2019, with low-interest rates and an improving economy, turns out to be a continuation of the last three quarters of 2017, we will see the whole industry expand faster, and the stable yield on dividend stocks will raise their values right away.

This is more important because we reflect on the other case: what if it goes the other direction and 2019, for economic or geopolitical purposes, or a mixture of both turned out to be a downer.

Then what happens to stocks with big dividends? Suppose you are early in your investing career and are seeking to develop a retirement portfolio. In that case, a downturn in the market offers you the opportunity to purchase quality stocks at a bargain price.

This is especially relevant if you implement a dollar-cost averaging system (regularly buying a certain dollar sum from a given stock or product) and have high yields on securities and reinvest dividends.

When you invest monthly, the cheaper your inventory, the more shares you purchase every month, and the dividend would maximize the annual return relative to a non-dividend paid growth stock.

On the continuum opposite end, you tend to collect the earnings stream as you withdraw and survive on dividends from your investments and keep high-quality dividend return securities irrespective of whether the price has increased or deteriorated.

Compare this to an investment plan focused on using a percentage of non-dividend paid income securities in an investment fund. Based on a forecast annual growth rate of 8%, it appeared appropriate to deduct 4% of sales each year.

The problem is that optimistic growth forecasts in the real world do not always come true.

If the market declined again in 2019, removing 4 percent could entail selling more stock than expected to sustain the income stream and reduce the potential retirement capacity. On the other hand, as you wait for a market rebound, the part of your portfolio that includes high-quality dividend stocks will continue to pay you at the same cost.

Although your net worth could be smaller, your revenue stream would remain unchanged (until the markets return).

Furthermore, if a dividend is paid, the company cannot stop if circumstances get bad.

A non-dividend spent business with a beautiful stock price appreciation will see it dropping just as rapidly if unexpected issues occur.

And how much of your portfolio will you spend on high-yield income stocks? This is a question that can only be resolved. It depends on a wide variety of factors, including your age, the amount of money you are expected to spend, the time you are prepared to invest to ensure that you have a portfolio with high return inventories with the highest quality, particularly your personal risk appetite and your investing style. Honestly, don't believe in a formula to decide what percentage a person would have in any market segment. Believe in conducting your work to ensure that you learn and appreciate the firms you invest in and why they demand better than average returns for high-income shares.

Be comfortable and ensure that the "good night's sleep" test is passed. When you're so concerned about your investments that you can't sleep, you don't spend on your risk appetite. While watching the talking heads on Television, I can testify to many analysts and political experts from all sides of the table. Others say the economy is going up, and others suggest it is going down. Some people are optimistic about the economy, and others fear like we are heading for another slump.

For the right blend of high- yield dividend-yielding equities as part of a diversified portfolio that fits your standards and risk appetite, you can be even better positioned to draw in for the future or whatever the future is, irrespective of the direction of stocks and you will depend on a disrupted income stream.

How To Pick Dividend Stocks And When To Buy?

Why does a stock slightly higher than other stocks yield a dividend? There could be many explanations.

High profits are also a symbol of high risk.

If the risk is actual or expected is a matter to be decided by each investor. Another factor could be the stock type.

If it is a Business Development Company, a Master Limited Partnership, or a Real Estate Investment Trust, the high dividend is partly due to government requirements that the vast majority of the earnings be passed on to stockholders to maintain a free corporate tax status.

A high yield may be due to the stock's price falling dramatically due to a general market slowdown, downturns in that particular industry, or unfortunate news for that specific company or shares with similar characteristics.

The yield decreases as the price declines, and the dividend remains the same.

Again, the real value of the individual stock under review may or may not reflect this.

Often that helps in the understanding of the product you are reviewing. Know the company, where it concerns its competition, and how it performs relative to previous quarters or years.

You should exclude it from the scanning system, whether you don't know what an organization does or do not appreciate what it does.

Price concern or period: The price of a stock is a very significant element in its choice.

Every commodity is up and down, regardless of whether the economy is up or down. Some of these improvements are driven by demand, and very particular steps influence others. Strong returns continue to fluctuate dramatically before and after the ex-dividend period. The crowd that catches distributions needs to get the payout.

Many that are interested in capital gains want to purchase and sell before the pre-ex-dividend climb.

Many buyers only want to buy before the payout, while others want to buy after the stock declines after the ex-dividend date. The price will also be profoundly influenced as a company purchases new inventories to raise funds.

Because MLPs, BDCs, and REITs tend to make much of their money, they also sell extra inventories to finance new production.

This is often viewed as a dilution, and after such an announcement, stock owners often sell this. The aim here is to see whether it is merely a dilution or whether future sales from growth funded by selling new shares would more than outweigh the increase of existing shares.

Perhaps the only way to do so is to see what happens before and to see what the company thinks it wants to do with the revenue from stock sales. Knowing the typical price cycle of a stock and its impacts is essential in terms of purchase timing.

Statistical metrics: Take a glance at stock benefit levels to see if a particular asset falls in.

When the PE is very high relative to other businesses, it raises a red flag. Likewise, if it's too low compared to equivalent machinery, why? A small PE caused by an irrationally low price is the way to look.

Metrics such as book price, purchase rates, cash flow rates should be analyzed in the historical sense of this particular product and within the market in which it operates.

Questions to ask: Is the dividend safe?

Is the payout entirely covered by revenue or cash flow?

Whose proportion of profits is paid in dividends?

It is necessary to know the company's debt to equity ratio in manufacturing companies.

Generally speaking, it is easier to have more equity than the debt that yields less than a shareholder liability ratio. Similarly, more existing assets than current liabilities are usually desirable, with the current rate of 2 or higher typically being a reasonable standard.

Such formulas do not explicitly illustrate REITs, MLP's, and BDC's, and issues such as the cash flow allocation, hedging, debt, curve of yield and rising interest rates are as significant or even more important consider.

Once, comprehension of the business under discussion also matters.

In calculating high returns, an organization's size is less important than its place among its competitors, its past success, and its anticipated results in the future. This is also clear that big, well-established businesses with long-term dividends are likely to be healthier than smaller, younger firms.

However, the latest Wall Street crash and other empires' fall show that what can appear dull is not, and what is historically stable will not be safe in the future.

Analysts: Most securities are evaluated by at least one analyst and often by five, four, or more. The opinion is based on moral concepts, scientific analysis, or a mixture of the two.

There is also a range of computerized analytical web tools such as MSN Monetary (free) and Value Line (fee) that link a stock metric to an "opinion" formulation. Analyst ratings are impressive because an analyst will often place a stock purchase rate, while another sells the same stock based on the same information. Looking at experts' views gives a valuable context evaluation and provides thought-provoking information, but they are not a replacement for your due diligence and personal appraisal.

Nobody knows what your standards are more than you for purchasing, selling, or holding stocks. Nobody knows better than you about your risk tolerance. No one knows how much more money you have to spend on a single market or resources than you. Although it is insightful to look at analyst reviews, note that they just have views, so your opinion will be as secure as or more durable than your own if you do the reading! Note, nobody cares more than you do about your money!

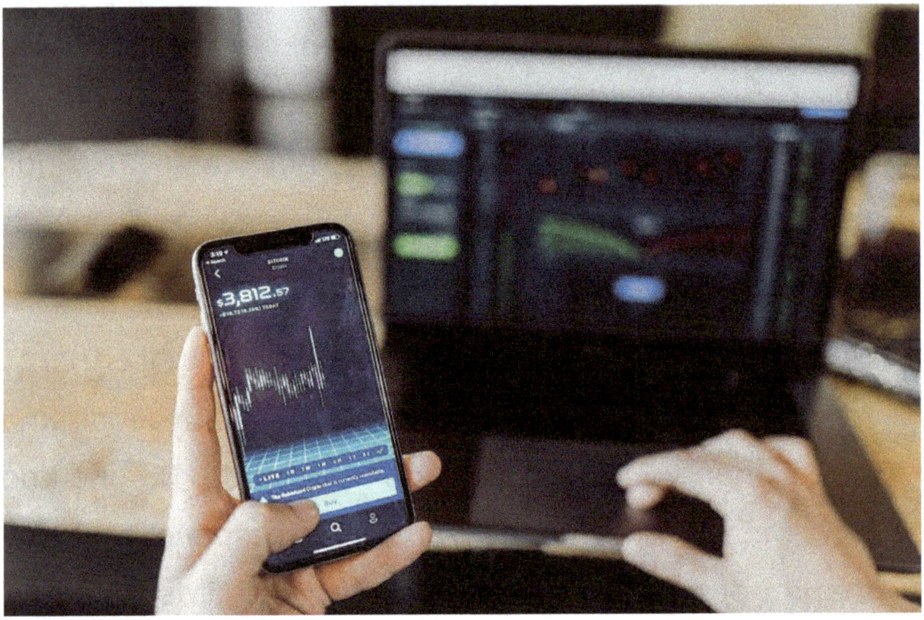
$3,812.57

Why Is The Dividend Investing Popular?

Once upon a time, people rarely traded in bonds. Bonds, bank accounts, and Guaranteed Investment Certificates were high income received, so that the buying of securities was not required.

With inflation and interest rates rising and long staying weak, people have been looking for other ways to generate money. The two most common approaches are real estate and dividend rent. Investment of real estate includes the purchase and sale of the property and is not addressed further. Dividend contributions will be discussed in this segment through the acquisition of shares.

When it comes to investing in dividends, there are some essential things to remember: profits are not promised.

Many Canadians are aware that shares and mutual funds are not protected until Canadian deposit insurance is adequate.

This is usually the case when bankrupt institutions hold your investments. The same happens to mutual securities as to shares. A business can alter or cancel its dividend payment entirely without much warning. This is usually announced at shareholders' meetings and by press releases. Companies that discard or reduce dividends indeed tend to receive poor advertising from the market, thus discouraging them, but it always happens. When profits are cut, they may change the course of the business.

One potential scenario is when a company decides to invest a lot of ongoing cash in a new product, new business line, or other company requiring money to grow it. Instead of paying dividends, the company has now decided to conserve its capital and allow the profits instead to generate capital gains. Secondly, the company does not make as much money as before and can no longer afford dividends.

A third scenario includes businesses with a negative shock such as a lawsuit, a policy reform that harms their business, a merger, a takeover, or a natural catastrophe that makes the corporation change its dividend course. Scenarios often occur where dividends rise more than anticipated, such as adding extra profits, a one-time dividend payout from a merger deal, the outcome of a dispute, and improvements in legislation that benefit the corporation and result in a substantial increase in profit. Read the media reports and decipher the current situation to find out what is happening to a company. May or may not keep up with inflation dividends.

This year, multiple businesses will increase dividends. In some cases, people believe it because it has been going on for many years.

These changes are intended to keep your dividend income stable as the product price falls, charging more dollars for each share of your stock. Such bigger payouts help keep inflation going and encourage your investment to retain its value for a long time. When the share price stagnates and dividend distributions are stable, inflation would not keep pace because you will get the same amount for several years.

Inflation would not deteriorate. As the price of goods increases, you will find that your money will buy less and less and will pinch cash. It is particularly relevant if the dividends are your only income stream or if you live on a fixed amount of money.

Most senior citizens and individuals with set government coverage are listed as such. To figure out what is happening in this situation, look at your business's dividend payment history and figure out if payment raises are planned. If they are often predictable, but there are some sudden pattern shifts, see what happened to the company at the moment.

Such intervals will decide how reliable the stock is and is not effective in the payment of dividends.

Dividend yields are influenced inversely by the price of the stock.

The amount of dividend dollars received at the time of dividend payment divided by the share price gives you a percentage called the "dividend yield."

This equation helps you equate this return with other assets, such as bond rates or GIC rates. The output can also be measured over time to see what the production will do. Since the stock price is the equation's denominator, the percentage given to you or the dividend yield will decline as the stock price rises.

Conversely, this dividend yield will increase as the stock price fell. That calculation would matter to you whether you invest for guaranteed profits and have shared, or if you want to change portfolios or need a certain amount of theory (money spent) for an option to dividend holding securities.

When you bring fresh capital into dividend options, this yield contrasts it with whether you have "cheap" (high yield) or "economic" (low return).

Many things affect the inventory price so that this yield will change significantly according to the inventory price at a particular time.

The dividend payment would not be very fluctuating unless something unusual occurs-as stated in the previous paragraphs.

How Is The Level Of Interest?

When trading in dividend pay-out securities, interest levels will be closely watched. The higher interest rates, the more probable it is that dividend options are issued because one will buy an option, shares, or other interest-bearing securities. It's like a substitute effect - if one thing becomes very costly and a cheaper version comes, you'll buy the more affordable version. If a dividend stock gives you a 5% income stream and a bond leaves you a 2% income stream, you will probably purchase the dividend stock after weighing risks, costs, and taxes. If the bond then provides you with a 4% income because of increased interest rates, this dividend stock is not attractive. If the relationship instead generates a revenue stream of 6 percent, it will already be a higher return than the stock paying dividends. People will sell the dividend stock before the price falls to approximately 6 percent or a corresponding return after risk, costs, and taxes. Because dividend payment will not adjust too quickly, the only solution to managing markets is to modify the price of the dividend stock in this situation.

Dividend Payment Process And how can you receive such dividends? The traditional method is to open a trading account with a bank or brokerage company. The statement must be such that you can purchase individual stocks. You can buy these products yourself, or anyone will buy them for you. Before setting up the account, make sure you ask questions about costs, account access limitations, and taxes. You will buy shares in each company. You would purchase 100 shares of Bell Canada Enterprises, for instance (the BCE trading symbol). Such investments will cost you an illustration of $50 per share. If you purchase 100 securities, $5,000 plus some stock will be paid. Many accounts do have costs to hold the wallet accessible but ask questions when buying products because such expenses can decrease the sum of money you earn from the entire process. You are entitled to a dividend payment every quarter once the shares are in your name.

The quarter-end date is the quarter-end date of the corporation, not the quarter-end date of the year. When you hold the stock that either the name or name of a mutual account listed with the Corporation, the name of the account owned by the securities would be set to collect the payout until the dividend payment date comes. You would earn the dividend if you bought shares before this date. You will instead see a cash payout for the stock in your portfolio. In some cases, the profits can be reinvested in more stocks rather than cash to ensure that you continue to buy more shares rather than yourself. This approach is useful if you want your inventory to expand. When you choose to invest your profits, you shouldn't do so because securities will be traded regularly to raise revenue, which will create some selling costs and expenses to plan the transactions and receive the best profit. This is difficult to time the business, and it cannot be ignored until you have any experience.

When Do You Not Have To Spend On Dividends?

The answer to this question depends on what your primary reasons for buying dividend returns and your risk tolerance are. If you just want money and can get your money by purchasing debt, the latter is a better choice. If you are incredibly risky to lose your capital, and a guaranteed alternative investment falls before you, you can instead purchase the guaranteed alternative. When you like dividend income, and like the capital gain that sometimes comes with it, you may want to retain your dividend balance even if other options are offered to you. When interest rates rise dramatically and you miss your earnings, the whole dividend investing principle can be switched off. If you value real estate and can produce a similar income from real estate against investing in dividends, real estate investment is the route for you because you know more about its functions.

Putting all this together, Investing in dividends should always be considered and everything else in your life, both financially and otherwise. Be mindful of what you want for dividend investing to achieve, your choices, and how confident you feel with each option. You will always recognize the amount of information you have about every opportunity. The more you learn about it, the smarter you are. Treat it as an exercise and gradually wade in for all that can be found before you learn a decent deal about it.

CPSIA information can be obtained
at www.ICGtesting.com
Printed in the USA
BVHW091641220421
605634BV00008B/819

9 781801 459266